Y0-EIZ-421

Copyright under USMC protection

Published by: Boulder Press LLC, P.O. Box 2001, Boulder, CO 80305
website: www.boulderpress.net

Photography and Text © 2008 Mike Barton

Individual prints may be purchased directly from the photographer: mikebartonphoto@yahoo.com, 720 934-4322 or via the website: www.mikebartonphoto.com.

No part of this book may be reproduced or transmitted in any form, including electronic or mechanical, without permission in writing from publisher.

ISBN 13: 978-0-9801024-1-3
ISBN 10: 0-9801024-1-3
First Printing: 2008
Created and designed in the United States.
Printed in Canada.

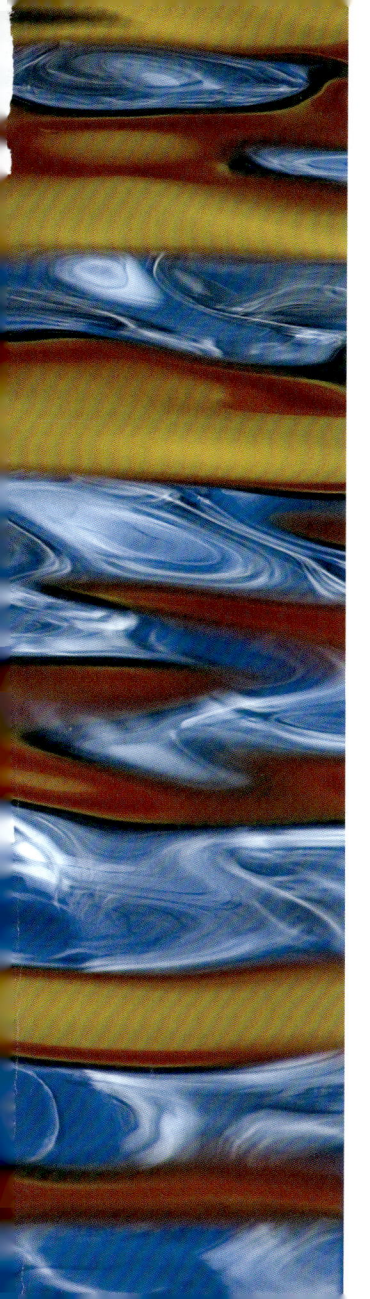

Charlevoix
The Beautiful

photography and text by Mike Barton

foreword by Sue Bolt

BOULDER PRESS

CHARLEVOIX

Foreword

I am not a writer, I am a painter but I will do my best to describe what is in my heart about the place where I live.

Northern Michigan has given me a gift of forever beauty. The four seasons are always surprises. The gentleness of summer days, magnificent sunsets, storms that well up over our lake and sky and make the water dance. The quietness of grey winter days with white snow that surrounds us. The fun of skaters and skiers, red cheeked from the cold. Warming by a log fire. Trilliums and mushrooms, spring beauties and bloodroot dot the forest floor. The canopies of trees with their fuzz of pale green as redwing blackbirds fly home to greet the summer.

A walk to the beach to find stones washed by the winter storms. The coldness of the water. Farms with green cornfields flowers as workers care for the earth. Bees, butterflies and other insects hum and sing, snakes, frogs, praying mantis all make up the wonder of a Michigan summer.

And when the bounty is bursting because of sun and water and wind, then comes the color and fruitfulness of Mother Earth and Father Sky. Giving us food for body and souls. This is where I live and my place in the world.

- Sue Bolt 2007

Charlevoix resident Sue Bolt is a renowned painter and owner of Bolts Grange Hall along with her husband Russ. In art school, Bolt majored in both sculpture and painting, so creating handmade ceramic tiles was a natural way to combine both of these talents.

CHARLEVOIX

Introduction

Charlevoix's unique charm makes it a popular destination for travelers from all over the world. In addition to the beautiful natural setting, the area offers wonderful restaurants, shopping, beaches, boating, golf, special events and breathtaking fall colors.

Charlevoix is one of the few remaining downtowns with an operating drawbridge. Stroll down Bridge Street filled with shops, fine dining and galleries while you enjoy the wonderful view of sailboats and yachts bobbing in the harbor.

The name "Charlevoix" comes from Pierre Francois Xavier de Charlevoix, a French priest who visited the area in 1721.

Take some time and explore neighboring cities such as Petoskey, Harbor Springs, Boyne and Traverse City.

The Emerald Isle enters the Pine River after a two-hour trip from Beaver Island.

INTRODUCTION

Sunrise stillness at the Round Lake Yacht Basin. A stroll along the harbor filled with boats never gets old.

Colorful Bridge Street is the heart of Charlevoix. At sunrise you can have the town all to yourself before the warm summer days bring out the crowds.

7

Boats come and go all day long.

INTRODUCTION

Sailboats flowing into Round Lake always make a great sight.

As the sun sinks into the great lake, many walk out onto the pier leading to the lighthouse.

INTRODUCTION

CHARLEVOIX
HAVE FUN OR DON'T

11

CHARLEVOIX

Bridge Street

Charlevoix is a lively place and Bridge Street is the center of attention. The charming downtown overlooks the huge green lawn of East Park and the picturesque, almost landlocked harbor on Round Lake.

Visitors stroll the tree-shaded sidewalks lined with restaurants, ice cream parlors, candy stores, coffee shops and all kinds of establishments from art galleries to antiques.

When you are shopped out or just want to take a break, find a place to rest your feet and soak up the sunshine while watching the passing spectacle.

CHARLEVOIX

Charlevoix resident vacuums the sidewalk with Magic (AKA Snake) and Bandit (AKA Beast).

Bridge Street is a great place for a stroll, window shopping or just hanging out for the day.

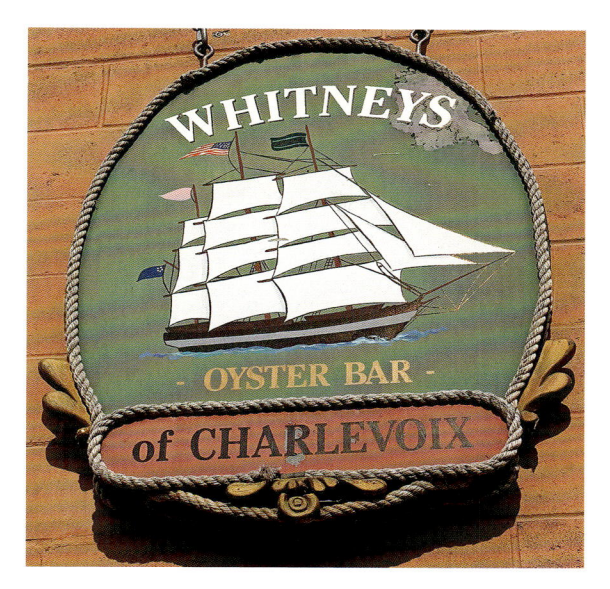

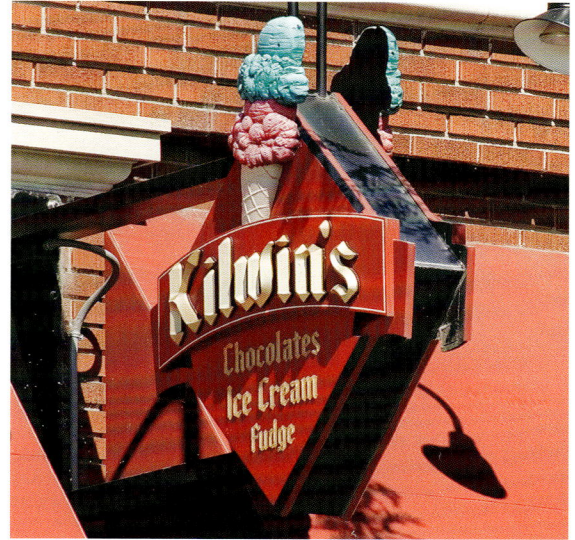

BRIDGE STREET

Go ahead and stop in for a box of fudge in the candy-filled storefront of Murdick's Famous Fudge.

Bridge Street hosts the farmers market every Thursday morning along side East Park.

BRIDGE STREET

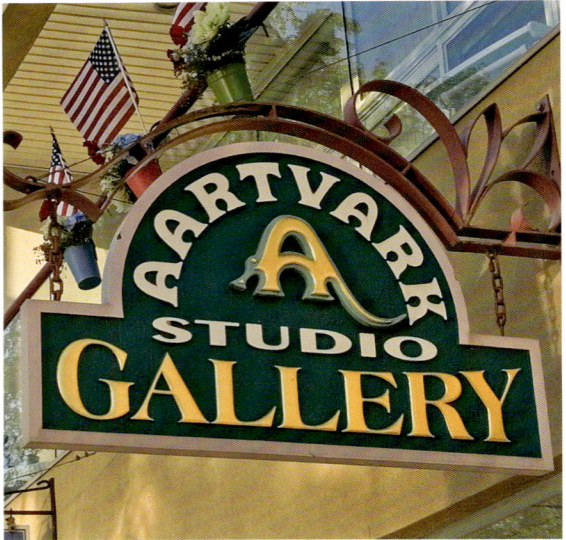

CHARLEVOIX

BRIDGE STREET

CHARLEVOIX

Joe and Sam Barton celebrate another "Kilwins Quest". Thanks Papa!

Quaint street-side cafes are found on every block on Bridge Street.

BRIDGE STREET

There's no shortage of ice cream on Bridge Street.

Kilwin's
Fudge
CE CREAM
Chocolates

WHITNEYS
Oyster Bar

MURD'ICKS
FAMOUS
FUDGE
OPEN

CHARLEVOIX

Round Lake Yacht Harbor

Hip Charlevoix is a harbor town and the Round Lake Yacht Basin is one of its treasured landmarks. The bowl-shaped Round Lake is surrounded by fancy boathouses and terraced ridges covered with stately homes.

Many people make a loop through the ever-lively Bridge Street and then take a peaceful stroll along the marina filled with yachts and sailboats.

Sailing through the harbor.

ROUND LAKE YACHT HARBOR

The huge lawn of East Park provides a relaxing setting to view the harbor.

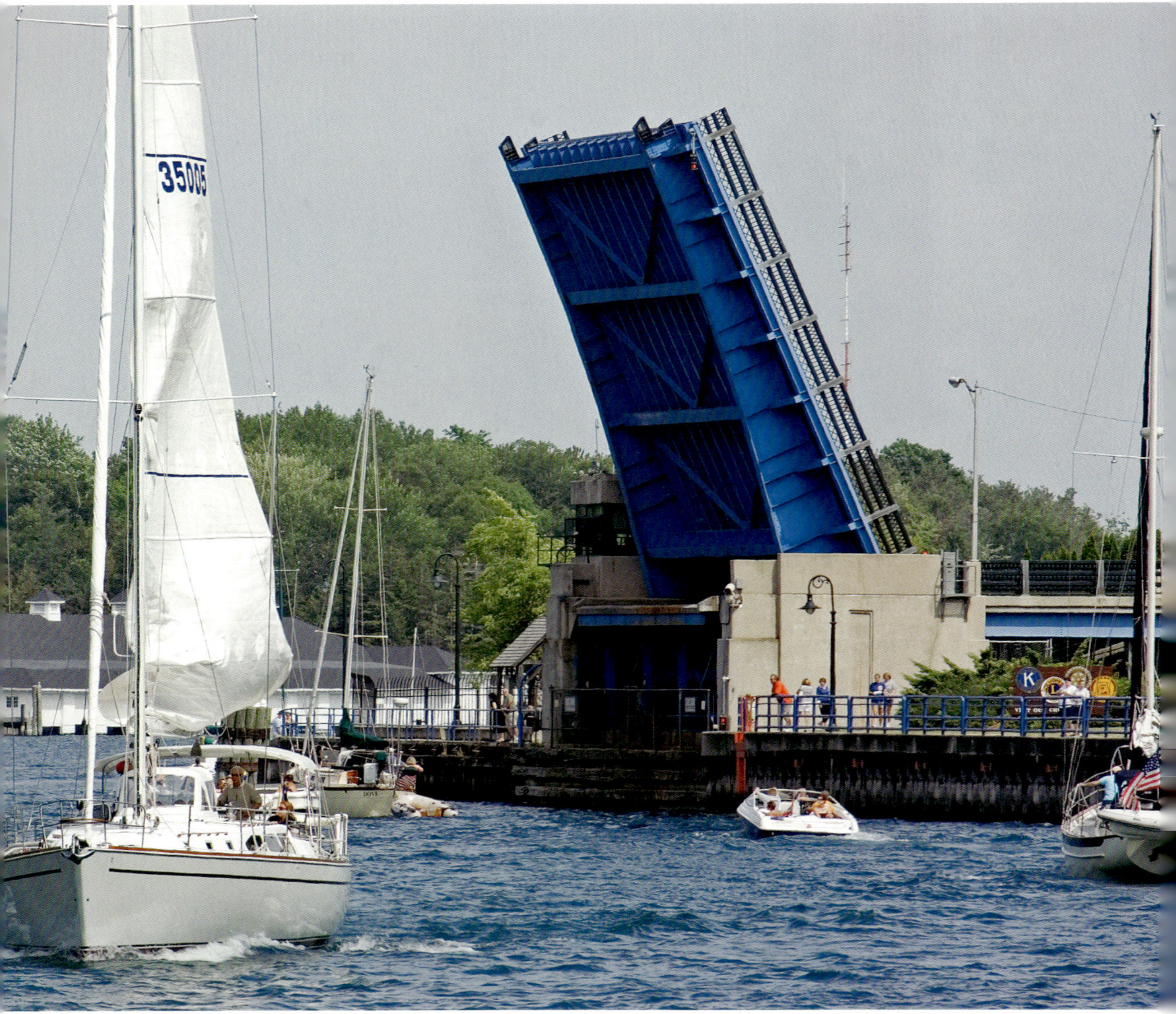
35005

MEMORIAL BRIDGE

The Memorial Bridge spanning the Pine River is Charlevoix's most notable landmark. This is the fifth bridge built over the Pine River. The first bridge was just a small wooden footbridge.

The drawbridge opens for boaters every half-hour and provides entertainment for spectators who gather to watch boats flow between the two raised halves. Even locals never seem to get tired of watching.

Charlevoix's answer to the Mackinac Bridge Walk is the "Little But Mighty Bridge Walk." The walk is held at noon every Labor Day, taking less than a minute for walkers to cross the short bridge.

The bridge was dedicated as the Charlevoix Memorial Bridge in 1949 to honor the men of Charlevoix who gave their lives during World War II.

CHARLEVOIX

MEMORIAL BRIDGE

CHARLEVOIX

CHARLEVOIX LIGHTHOUSE

The Charlevoix Lighthouse is located on the south pier at the end of the Pine River, marking the entrance to Round Lake and Lake Charlevoix from Lake Michigan. The current structure replaced the original wooden structure in 1948.

For such a plain looking lighthouse, it is surprisingly very photogenic, thanks to the sleek profile of the south pier and beautiful background sunsets.

The lighthouse greets arriving boaters.

CHARLEVOIX LIGHTHOUSE

Long exposure captures a boat light trail heading out to Lake Michigan.

CHARLEVOIX

After midnight, the Big Dipper hovers over the Charlevoix Lighthouse.

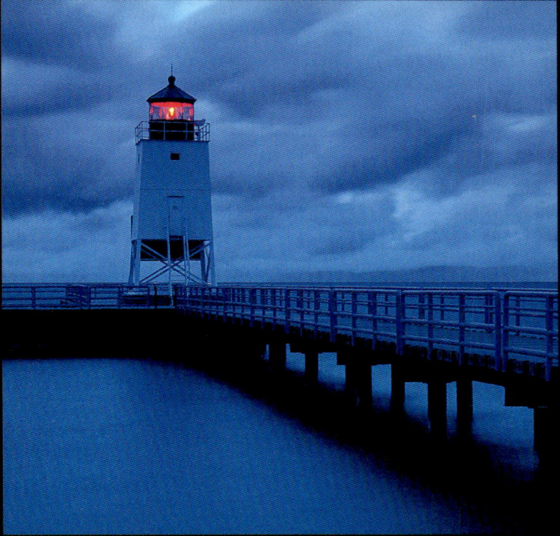
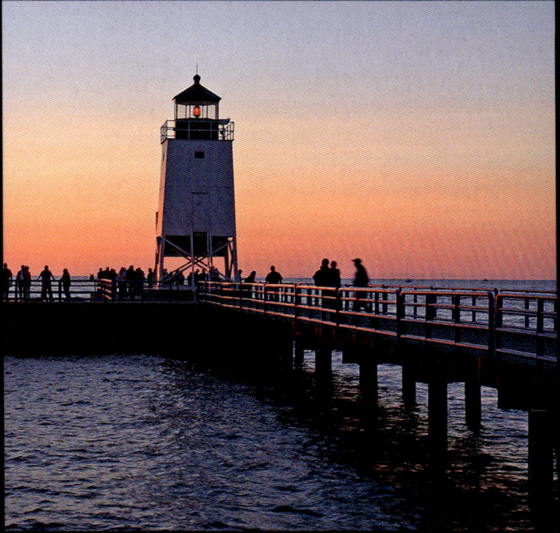
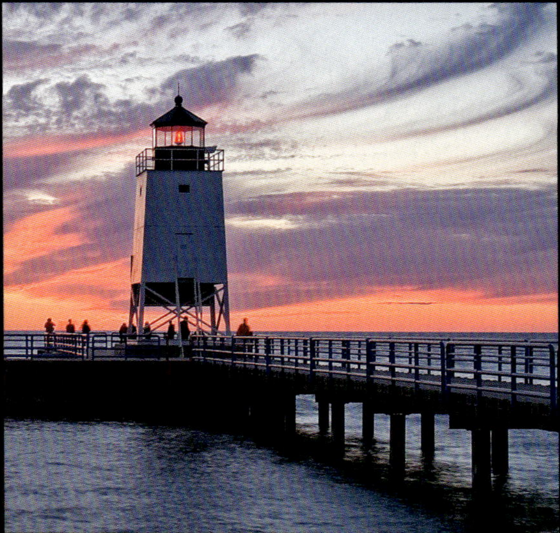
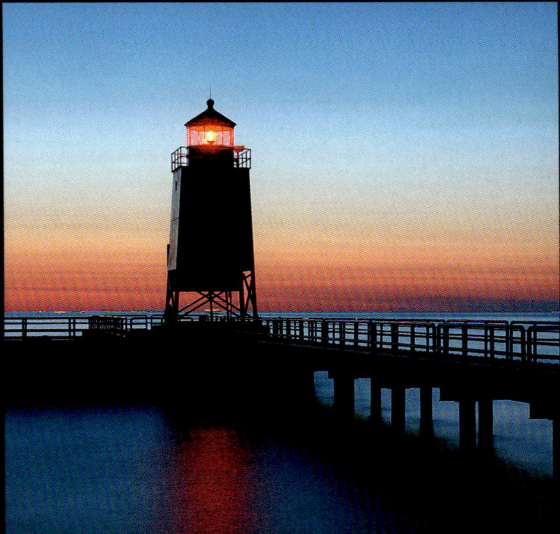

CHARLEVOIX

BEACHES

Just a short walk from downtown is white sand Lake Michigan Beach. Children play on playground equipment while adults soak up the sun and hunt for Petoskey stones along the shoreline. The beach is also a favorite spot to watch stunning sunsets over Lake Michigan.

Located on the west shore of Lake Charlevoix, Depot Beach usually has calmer and warmer water than Lake Michigan Beach. The historic Charlevoix Train Depot is located just behind the beach.

Twilight at Depot Beach, across from the historic Charlevoix Train Depot on Lake Charlevoix

This bagpipe player often performs on Lake Michigan Beach during sunset.

CHARLEVOIX

Sunset doesn't stop kids from going for a spin on the beach.

Sunrise at Depot Beach.

Petoskey stone washes up on Lake Michigan Beach.

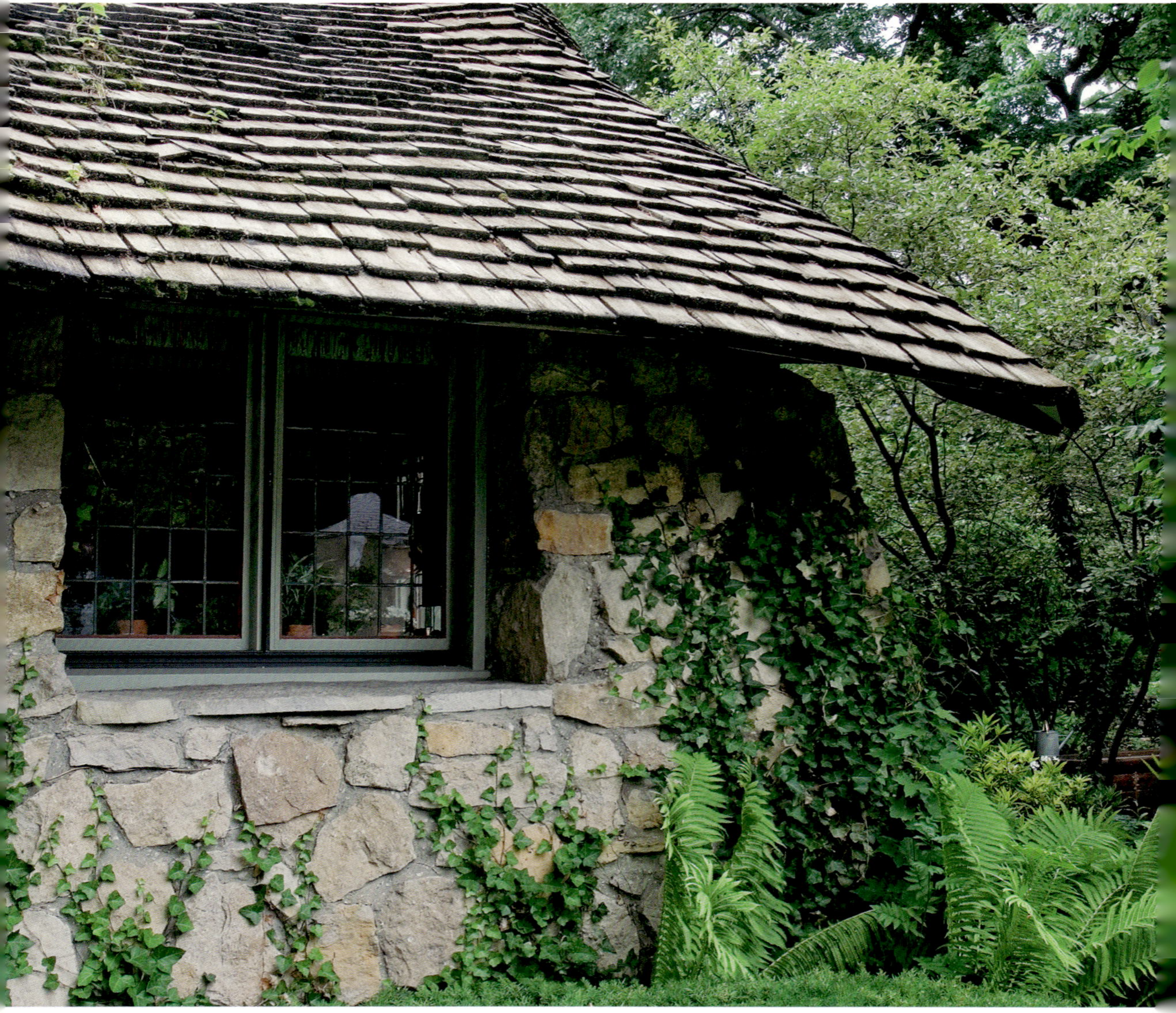

Earl Young Stone Houses

Without using a blueprint, Earl Young used his great imagination to design these irregular shaped houses with wave-like rooflines and intricate stonework. Many people say they look like something out of J.R.R. Tolkein's "The Hobbit."

Young moved to Charlevoix when he was ten years old and began to collect stones along the lakeshore, quarries and fields. Many of the stones used to build these legendary houses came from his lifelong passion of collecting stones.

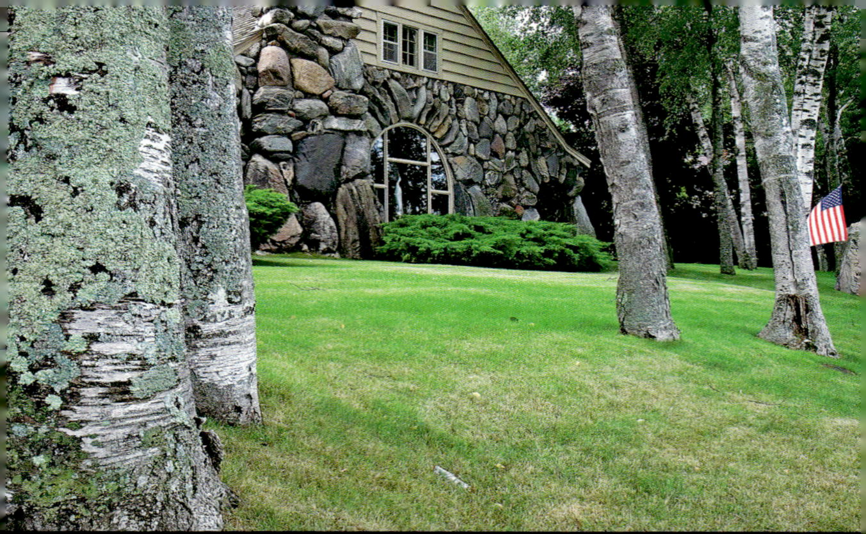

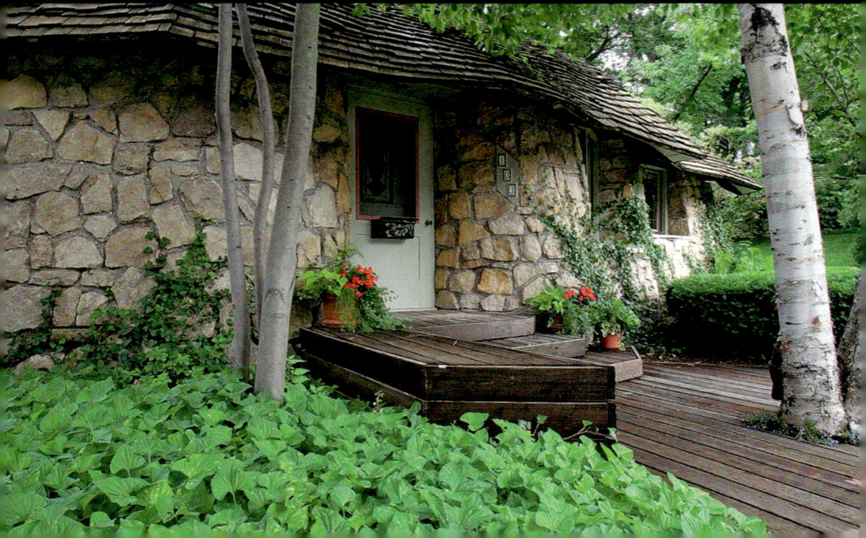

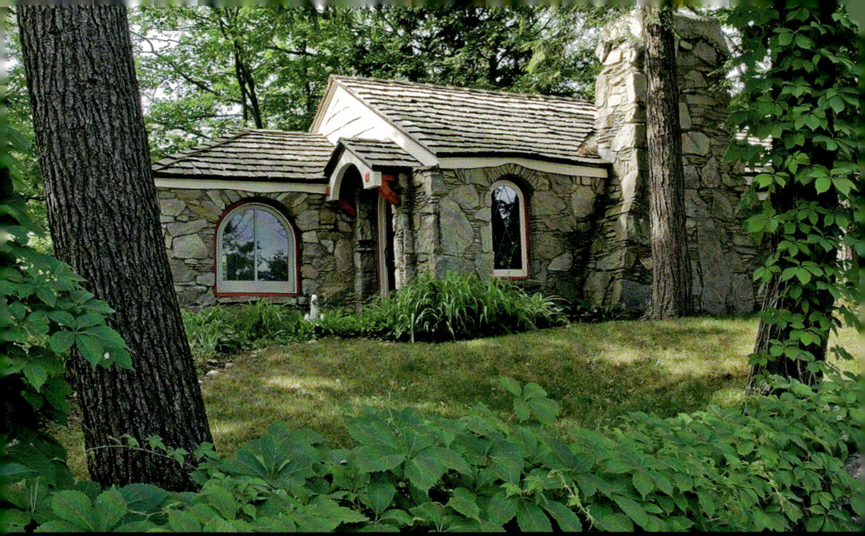

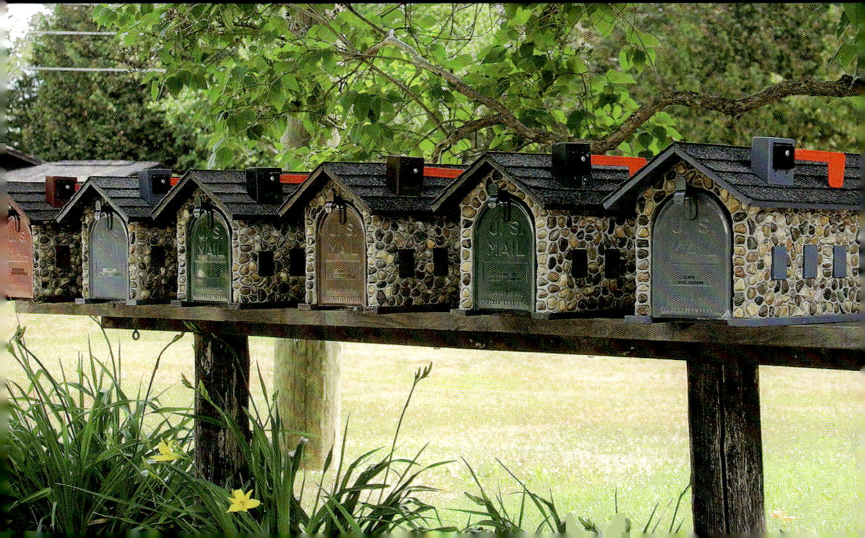

CHARLEVOIX

Around Town

Discovering Charlevoix's beauty and charm is easy because it's all within walking distance of downtown. Explore the tree-lined neighborhoods with unique architecture, sandy beaches, shops and cafes.

The Charlevoix Historical Society located in the Harsha House Museum will help give you an understanding of the special sense of place and character that Charlevoix offers.

ABOVE: The Charlevoix Historical Society and Harsha House Museum are located in a restored Victorian home.

LEFT: Charlevoix United Methodist Church.

Trademark stone work of lengendary architect Earl Young can be found west of downtown.

CHARLEVOIX

The meticulously restored Train Depot was donated to the Charlevoix Historical Society in June 1992, the 100th anniversary of the arrival of the first passenger train to visit Charlevoix.

The Weathervane is Charlevoix's most unique restaurant. Designed by Earl Young, the restaurant has an unobstructed view of sailboats and yachts in the channel below.

AROUND TOWN

ABOVE: Golf legends such as Walter Hagen and Tommy Armour have teed it up at the Charlevoix Golf Course - The Muni. The course is one of the oldest in Michigan, opening in 1896.

LEFT: A dazzling display of petunias welcome visitors entering downtown Charlevoix. In 1982, a group called Keep Charlevoix Beautiful launched "Operation Petunia." Every year, hundreds of volunteers show up on the Thursday before Memorial Day weekend to plant petunias along the five miles of roadway from city limit to city limit.

AROUND TOWN

CHARLEVOIX

Venetian Festival

What began in 1930 as a parade of boats with candle-lit paper lanterns to celebrate the end of the sailing regattas has grown into a weeklong festival that attracts thousands of visitors. It takes about 300 volunteers each year to run this huge event that includes fireworks, carnival rides, craft shows, music, sporting competitions and a rodeo.

The magical boat parade in Round Lake is still the heart of the Venetian Festival. After the sun goes down, the water in the harbor begins to shimmer from the reflective glow of decorated boats of all shapes and sizes as they circle Round Lake. Fireworks begin to light up the sky as the last boat passes through the harbor.

CHARLEVOIX

BACK ROADS

Escape the crowds and take an afternoon to discover the farms, forests, lakes and small towns surrounding Charlevoix the Beautiful. There are many places to explore along the back road areas within a half hour drive from downtown. Don't forget to come back in October to view the spectacular Northern Michigan autumn colors.

CHARLEVOIX

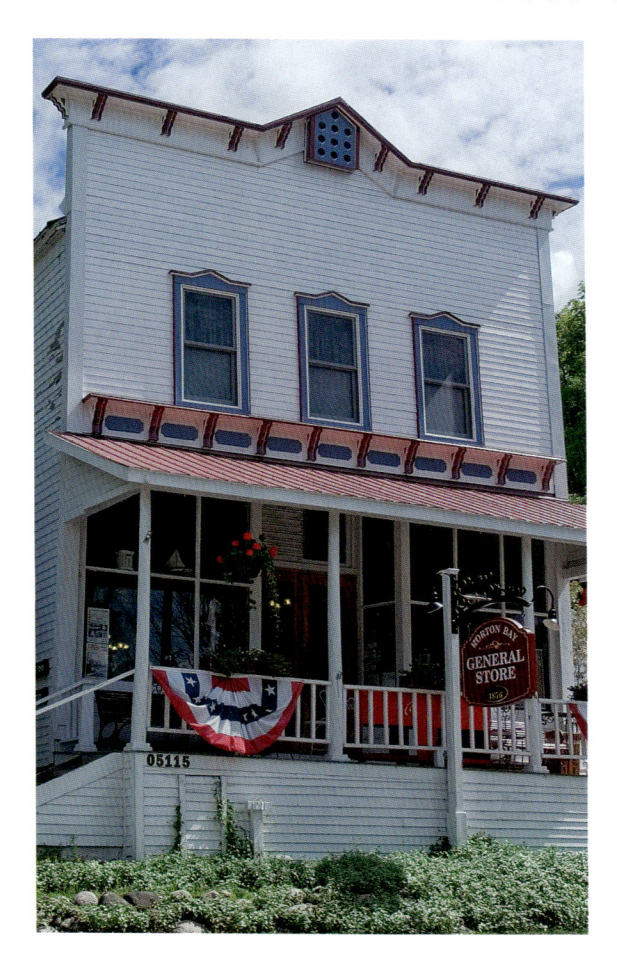

ABOVE: The historic General Store in Horton Bay was frequented by Earnest Hemmingway, who spent his summers at nearby Walloon Lake.

RIGHT: Horton Bay is tucked along the west shore of Lake Charlevoix.

Purple Coneflowers dress up old farm equipment.

Sunflowers along highway US 31.

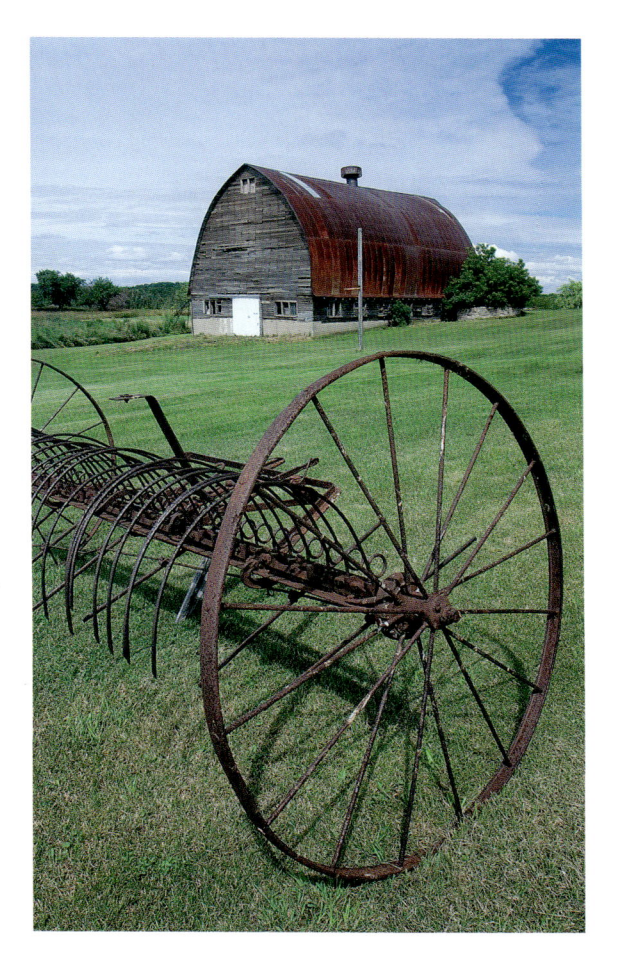

ABOVE: Evidence of a once thriving farming community is sprinkled all around the outskirts of Charlevoix the Beautiful.

RIGHT: Bike trails can be found just north of town at the 50-acre recreation area at Mount McSauba.

About The Photographer

Mike Barton is a landscape photographer from Boulder, Colorado. Born and raised in Michigan, Mike earned an engineering degree from Michigan State and immediately headed west and settled in California for 17 years.

Mike has accumulated dozens of photographic credits, including covers, and has sold over 1,000 prints. His work is selling at several locations in Colorado and over the Internet.

Mike's style has been characterized by the vibrant contrasting colors that evoke a sense of energy and joy. It is not unusual to find Mike out shooting well before the sunrise and out past dark, often waiting hours for the ideal conditions or moments.

The over 120 photographs in this book were taken in just two-one week vacations in 2004 and 2007 while visiting his parents, both residents of Charlevoix. (Thanks Mom and Dad!)

Thanks

Many thanks to the people who shared their time, support and encouragement.

Greg and Suzanne Barton for their ideas. Nephews Sam and Joe Barton for making my visits to Charlevoix extra fun. To my parents Graham and Betty - thanks for living in Charlevoix the Beautiful and letting me stop by every summer.

Venetian Festival photos courtesy of Laurie Hodgson of North Bays Design Group.